Thanksgiving Turkeys

BY PATRICK MERRICK

The Child's World®

Published by The Child's World®
1980 Lookout Drive • Mankato, MN 56003-1705
800-599-READ • www.childsworld.com

ACKNOWLEDGMENTS

The Child's World®: Mary Berendes, Publishing Director
The Design Lab: Design
Olivia Gregory: Editing
Pamela J. Mitsakos: Photo Research

Design elements ©: Sashkin/Shutterstock.com: utensils
Photographs ©: Andrei Rybachuk/Shutterstock.com: 19;
Botond Horvath/Shutterstock.com: 5; evgenyb/iStock.com:
13, 21; Gordo25/iStock.com: 6-7; javarman/Shutterstock.
com: 4-5; Jeff Banke/Shutterstock.com: cover, 1; Jennie
Augusta Brownscombe/Wikimedia Commons: 11; Joseph
Andrews/Wikimedia Commons: 9; Lois_McCleary/iStock.
com: 16-17; PaulTessier/iStock.com: 15

ISBN 9781631437472
LCCN 2014945401

Printed in the United States of America
Mankato, MN
November, 2014

Table of Contents

Meet the Thanksgiving Turkey!

Fall is a great time of year! The leaves change color. The air turns crisp and cool. Farmers pick vegetables and gather grains. On a special fall **holiday** called Thanksgiving, we give thanks for the good things in our lives. One thing to be thankful for is the Thanksgiving turkey!

You know fall has arrived when the leaves turn yellow and orange. Trees look beautiful when this happens.

What Is Thanksgiving?

Thanksgiving is held around the time that farmers finish **harvesting** their crops in late fall. It is on the fourth Thursday of November in the United States. Thanksgiving in Canada is on the second Monday of October. This is because the harvest is earlier there.

Farmers usually finish harvesting around the time of Thanksgiving. Then we get to eat all of the delicious things they grew!

Do Many People Celebrate Thanksgiving?

Most parts of the world have special days for giving thanks. The United States was the first country to have an official Thanksgiving Day. European settlers had a difficult time when they came to North America. One reason we celebrate Thanksgiving is to remember those settlers.

The first Thanksgiving happened soon after the first settlers arrived in North America.

What Was the First Thanksgiving Like?

People called **Pilgrims** sailed from England to North America nearly 400 years ago. They had a hard time finding food until a Native American named Squanto taught them how.

The Pilgrims held a huge feast to celebrate. They invited the Native Americans who helped them. We now have Thanksgiving to honor the early settlers and those who helped them.

The Pilgrims sailed to North America on the *Mayflower*. They left England so they could practice their religion freely.

What Is the Thanksgiving Turkey?

Food is an important part of Thanksgiving. Most families have a big meal in the middle of the day. They might eat corn, sweet potatoes, pumpkin pie, or other tasty foods. The main dish is usually a big, juicy roasted turkey!

Many people eat turkey on Thanksgiving. It is often the main food for the holiday.

Why Do We Eat Turkey?

Turkey has been a part of Thanksgiving since the days of the Pilgrims. This is because turkey is **native** to North America. There were a lot of wild turkeys when the Pilgrims started hunting for food in their new home. We eat turkey on Thanksgiving because people ate it at the first Thanksgiving.

Turkeys were an important food for the Pilgrims. Hunting the wild turkeys helped feed the Pilgrims.

What Is a Wild Turkey?

The Pilgrims found wild turkeys all over eastern North America. So many people hunted wild turkeys that they almost became **extinct**.

People today have been trying to bring wild turkeys back. Now you can find wild turkeys in almost every state. Most people now eat farm turkeys instead of hunting wild turkeys.

It is easy to find turkeys in the wild today. You might have even seen one yourself.

What Is a Farm Turkey?

People started catching wild turkeys and raising them on farms a long time ago. These farm turkeys do not look much like wild ones any more. Farm turkeys are much bigger and cannot fly.

Almost 300 million farm turkeys are raised every year. Most of them are eaten on Thanksgiving and Christmas.

Farm turkeys look a lot different from wild ones. Many people think farm turkeys taste better than wild turkeys.

How Do We Eat Turkey?

There are many different recipes for Thanksgiving turkey. You can barbecue it, roast it, or make soup with it.

The turkey has become a **symbol** of Thanksgiving. It helps us remember the Pilgrims and all the things we are thankful for.

Many people stuff the turkey with other tasty foods before cooking it.

GLOSSARY

extinct (ek-STINGKT) When a kind of animal becomes extinct, there aren't any more of those animals left. Wild turkeys were once in danger of becoming extinct.

harvesting (HAR-veh-sting) When farmers harvest crops, they pick them. Most farmers harvest their crops in the fall.

holiday (HOL-uh-day) A holiday is a special day that people celebrate every year. Thanksgiving is a holiday.

native (NAY-tiv) A native is a person, animal, or plant that still lives in the place where it was born. Wild turkeys are native to North America.

Pilgrims (PIL-gruhmz) The Pilgrims were the first people who left England to live in North America. The Pilgrims celebrated the first Thanksgiving.

symbol (SIM-bul) A symbol is an object that is used to stand for something else. The turkey is a symbol of Thanksgiving.

BOOKS AND WEB SITES

BOOKS

Arnosky, Jim. *All about Turkeys*. New York: Scholastic, 1998.

Heiligman, Deborah. *Celebrate Thanksgiving with Turkey, Family, and Counting Blessings.* Washington, D.C.: National Geographic Children's Books, 2006.

Kamma, Anne. *If You Were At The First Thanksgiving.* New York: Scholastic, 2001.

Randall, Ronne. *Thanksgiving Sweets and Treats.* New York: Windmill Books, 2013.

WEB SITES

Visit our Web site for lots of links about Thanksgiving turkeys:

childsworld.com/links

Note to Parents, Teachers, and Librarians: We routinely verify our Web links to make sure they are safe, active sites—so encourage your readers to check them out!

INDEX

ABOUT THE AUTHOR

Patrick Merrick was born in California and spent much of his early life moving from town to town and from state to state. Eventually, his family settled in Sioux Falls, South Dakota. In addition to writing more than 45 children's books, Patrick has been teaching science to children for more than a decade. Patrick lives in southern Minnesota with his wife and five children. When not busy with school, writing, or parenting, Patrick enjoys the occasional nap.